Early Canada
Fur Traders

Heather C. Hudak

Editor

Weigl

CALGARY

www.weigl.com

Published by Weigl Educational Publishers Limited
6325 10 Street SE
Calgary, Alberta, Canada
T2H 2Z9

Website: www.weigl.com
Copyright ©2007 Weigl Educational Publishers Limited

Library and Archives Canada Cataloguing in Publication Data

Fur traders / editor, Heather Hudak.

(Early Canada)
Includes index.
ISBN 1-55388-238-5 (bound)
ISBN 1-55388-239-3 (pbk.)

1. Fur trade—Canada—History—Juvenile literature.
I. Hudak, Heather C., 1975– II. Series: Early Canada (Calgary, Alta.)
FC3207.H74 2006   j381'.43970971   C2006-902485-5

Printed in Canada
1 2 3 4 5 6 7 8 9 0   10 09 08 07 06

We acknowledge the financial support of the Government of Canada through the Book Publishing Industry Development Program (BPIDP) for our publishing activities.

Photograph and Text Credits
Every reasonable effort has been made to trace ownership and to obtain permission to reprint copyright material. The publishers would be pleased to have any errors or omissions brought to their attention so that they may be corrected in subsequent printings.

Cover: Library and Archives Canada; **Archives of Ontario Library:** page 16; **Library and Archives Canada:** pages 1, 24 ("Kelsey on the Plains" by Rex Woods 1957 (oil 43 x 33). Reproduced with the permission of Rogers Communications Inc.), 26, 27, 30, 36, 38, 43; **Mary Evans Picture Library:** pages 23, 31; **North Wind Picture Archives:** pages 23, 31.

Project Coordinator
Leia Tait

Designer
Warren Clark

All of the Internet URLs given in the book were valid at the time of publication. However, due to the dynamic nature of the Internet, some addresses may have changed, or sites may have ceased to exist since publication. While the author and publisher regret any inconvenience this may cause readers, no responsibility for any such changes can be accepted by either the author or the publisher.

Contents

4   **Introduction**

6   **European Interest in North America**

8   **In Search of Furs**

10   **A Montagnais Visits Tadoussac**

12   **Fur Trade Landmarks**

14   **Champlain and the Fur Trade**

16   **The Fur Trade Wars**

18   **The Company of One Hundred Associates**

20   **Aboriginal Women in the Fur Trade**

22   **Groseilliers and Radisson**

24   **Henry Kelsey**

26   **Pierre de La Vérendrye**

28   **The Nor'Westers**

30   **The Life of a Voyageur**

32   **Samuel Hearne**

34   **Alexander Mackenzie**

36   **People with Different Ideas**

38   **Simon Fraser**

40   **The Decline of the Fur Trade**

42   **Timeline**

44   **Research Activity: Adam Dollard: An Unselfish Hero?**

45   **Creative Activity: Reliving the Past**

46   **Further Research**

47   **Glossary**

48   **Index**

Introduction

Canada is a large country with several geographic regions. The climate, land, and **resources** of these areas shaped the experiences of early traders who explored the wilderness in search of furs. Their ventures opened the country's interior for **settlement** and created Canada's first major economic activity—the fur trade. They also helped form co-operative relationships between Europeans and **Aboriginal Peoples**.

Learning about people and events in Canada's history can help people better understand the country today. However, finding out what happened in the past and why it happened can be a challenge. In order to study the past, historians must piece together history from many different sources. Sometimes, they listen to the stories people tell. Often, they read historical **documents**. Many men who joined the fur trade in early Canada wrote about their experiences in journals or letters to family and friends. They also left behind trade documents, such as lists of supplies, trade receipts, and maps of trade routes and lands. Some of these documents still exist. From these records, historians can

Before the fur trade began, Aboriginal Peoples made most of their weapons, including arrowheads, from stone.

learn about the fur trade and its participants.

Without cameras, fur traders in early Canada relied on their own artistic skills to depict the new people and places they saw. They sketched the plants and animals they found in the Canadian interior. Sometimes, traders included themselves in their drawings. These images can tell historians a great deal about the activities and views of fur traders in early Canada.

Historians and archaeologists also study objects from the past to learn more about the people who made and used them. Trapping equipment and trade goods that have survived over time can reveal important facts about the day-to-day lives of fur traders in early Canada.

Learning about the past is a bit like putting a puzzle together. Pieces of information from different sources fit together to form a picture. Sometimes pieces are missing, so the picture is not complete. Then, historians must try to guess what really happened.

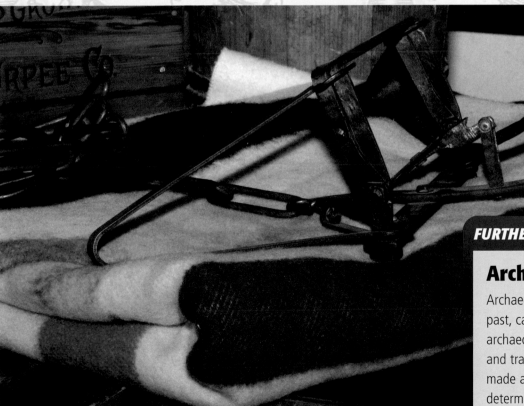

Point blankets were important European trade items during the fur trade. They are still made today.

European Interest in North America

Early contacts between Aboriginal Peoples and Europeans quickly came to involve the exchange of goods.

Early European explorers traded goods with the Aboriginal Peoples they met.

In the 1400s, explorers from Portugal, Spain, France, and Great Britain took to the oceans in search of an easier route to Asia. They were sent by **monarchs** and **merchants** who wanted better access to the spices, silks, and jewels found there. Some of these explorers believed that they would find a route to Asia by sailing west across the Atlantic Ocean. Instead, they discovered a whole new land.

North America was not a land of silks or spices, but it was rich in other resources. The waters off its eastern coast were teeming with fish. Early explorers returned to Europe with tales of waters so thick with fish, sailors could walk across them. Soon, fishers from all over Europe were heading to the new lands each spring, fishing for cod in areas known as the **Grand Banks**.

Sometimes these sailors and early explorers ventured ashore to look for supplies and set up camp. There, they met Aboriginal Peoples who lived near the shore. Soon after Europeans made contact with Aboriginal Peoples, they began to exchange goods. Aboriginal Peoples proved eager to the obtain Europeans goods. They offered European fishers animal furs and fresh meat in exchange for metal fish hooks, knives, axes, cooking pots, and other goods.

Aboriginal Peoples liked the goods they obtained from European fishers. Groups began travelling to the coast each summer to meet the fishing boats and conduct trade.

FURTHER UNDERSTANDING

Aboriginal Peoples

Aboriginal Peoples were the first people to live in North America. They believe their ancestors have always lived in Canada. Scientists believe that the Aboriginal Peoples are descended from ancient peoples who travelled to North America from Asia thousands of years ago. As groups settled in different regions of the continent, they adapted to their surroundings. By the time Europeans arrived, many different groups lived all over North America. Each group had its own way of life, its own language, its own spiritual beliefs, and its own laws.

FIRST-HAND ACCOUNT

Cartier Trades with the Mi'kmaq

Jacques Cartier was the first French explorer to come ashore in North America. In 1534, he made make a detailed exploration of Canada's east coast, exploring the Gulf of St. Lawrence and visiting what are now Prince Edward Island and New Brunswick. During his voyage, Cartier became the first European to record an act of trade with Aboriginal Peoples.

On July 6, 1534, Cartier met a group of Mi'kmaq people at their summer fishing camp. The Mi'kmaq had seen European ships before. They made signs to show that they were eager to trade with the Europeans. Cartier stopped his boats and traded items with the group. He recorded the details of the encounter in his journal:

"Nine canoes came to our ship. We rowed out to meet them in two longboats. They made signs to show that they wanted to trade. They held up some furs and clothing. We sent two men on shore with knives, iron goods, and a red cap for their chief. Before long, they brought their furs over.

"They showed great pleasure in obtaining our iron wares and other items. They danced and performed many ceremonies, and threw salt water over their heads with their hands.

"We soon traded for all the furs they had. They bartered all they had to such an extent that they all went back naked without anything on them. They made signs to us that they would return the next day with more furs.

"While sailing [the next day], we saw another group on the shore of a lake. We directed our boats down a channel flowing into the lake and went ashore. Seeing this, the Aboriginal people held up some pieces of seal meat and made signs to show that they wished to give it to us. We sent two men to them with hatchets, knives, beads, and other items to trade. This made them very happy. They began coming to us in groups, bringing furs and animal skins to trade in exchange for our wares."

Cartier traded with Aboriginal Peoples during his first voyage to Canada.

In Search of Furs

The beaver is Canada's largest rodent. Its fur was valued as a decorative clothing material.

When fishers and early explorers returned to Europe from North America, they brought back the furs they had obtained from trading with Aboriginal Peoples. Fur was needed in Europe to make hats and other clothing items. The furs from Canada, especially beaver **pelts**, were very easy to sell in Europe. Some individuals quickly realized that they could make a great deal of money this way. They began to travel to Canada just to trade for furs. Some fishers stopped fishing and became full-time fur traders.

The trade in furs grew quickly. In their brief explorations of the Atlantic coast, European fishers had discovered the St. Lawrence River. French fur traders began travelling farther up the river to trade furs with Aboriginal groups. These traders claimed the land for France so that no one else could trade for furs in the region. Merchants in France decided to create companies to collect furs on this land, which they called New France. In 1600, a wealthy merchant named Pierre de Chauvin travelled to the St. Lawrence region in order to build a fur trade post and **colony**. For his settlement, Chauvin chose Tadoussac, a favorite spot for European fur traders and fishers. Tadoussac was located at the junction of the Saguenay and St. Lawrence Rivers, in present-day

FURTHER UNDERSTANDING

New France

France's colonies in North America were called New France. Jacques Cartier took possession of the area for France in 1534. Samuel de Champlain created French settlements there in 1608. Gradually, settlers came to fish and work in the fur trade. **Missionaries** also came.

Beaver pelts

Beaver fur from Canada was very high quality. Canada's cold winters made the fur grow long and thick. In Europe, both the French and British used furs, especially from beavers, to make hats and to decorate other clothing. Beaver furs were an excellent trade product because they were unavailable in Europe, where the beaver was almost **extinct**. Pelts were also easily transported, even over long distances.

Quebec. The area had long been an important summer trading spot for the local Montagnais people. Aboriginal trade routes led from Tadoussac into the interior. Chauvin thought the area would be ideal to trade with the Montagnais all year. The trading post was built, and the colonists spent the summer trading for beaver pelts with the Montagnais. When autumn arrived, Chauvin and many of the colonists returned to France with their cargo of furs. Sixteen traders remained at the trading post through the winter. Only five survived. The cold, snowy Canadian winters were too harsh for the European colonists, and the settlement failed.

The Importance of Trade in Aboriginal Society

Long before Europeans came to North America, trade was an important part of life for Aboriginal Peoples. Neighbouring groups shared complex trading partnerships with one another. At specific times of the year, they gathered at chosen locations to trade items such as tobacco, maize, and copper—the only metal Aboriginal Peoples possessed before contact with Europeans.

Trade was accompanied by special ceremonies, feasting, and gift-giving. These activities indicated that trade in Aboriginal society was not just a means of obtaining goods. It was also an important social

Aboriginal Peoples traded corn and squash with fur traders.

custom. Trade renewed community bonds, brought groups together, and solidified political ties.

Trade also helped determine an individual's place in the community. In Aboriginal society, the most respected individuals were not those who collected vast amounts of goods and wealth for themselves. Rather, the most respected members of a community were those who shared their belongings with others. Sharing was a way of life for Aboriginal Peoples. If one person obtained many goods through trade, he or she shared these items with community members. Selfishness and hoarding were shunned. In this way, trade provided Aboriginal Peoples with the opportunity to demonstrate their generosity, a trait that was highly valued in Aboriginal society.

A MONTAGNAIS VISITS TADOUSSAC

The Montagnais began trading with Europeans at Tadoussac around 1600. This story tells what it might have been like when Aboriginal Peoples and Europeans began trading. What changes did the fur trade bring to Aboriginal Peoples' lives?

> Tadoussac, the meeting place by the two rivers, was now a year-round trading place.

Winter was very fine this year. About 40 of my people hunted together all winter. In the spring, we travelled to our summer camp. Most of the band was already there, so we soon set out for the large meeting place on the coast where we usually spent the summer. On the coast, there were many Naskapi people from the North, and there were Cree and Algonquin people from the East, as well as many of our Montagnais. As usual, we had a good time talking and playing games. The weather had been good. Most people were healthy and had many things to trade.

My mother wanted to find some metal knives. She had heard that there were foreigners on the coast with knives to trade. Some Algonquin people heard us talking, and they showed us some metal goods they had. They wanted to trade with us, but would only take beaver skins. We did not have many skins. Beavers are not that useful to us—not like caribou.

Some other families said that Tadoussac, the meeting place by the two rivers, was now a year-round trading place. There were foreigners there, they said, with many trading goods. The Algonquin traders were angry because they wanted us to trade with them. My father just laughed. We would get busy trapping beavers, he said, and then take a trip to Tadoussac ourselves.

All the adults in our group agreed this would be a good idea. We set off to the southeast, stopping to trap beavers along the way. As we got closer to Tadoussac, we met more and more people who wanted to trade goods for our beaver skins.

When we arrived at Tadoussac, there were people everywhere. We saw many foreigners wearing strange clothes. To our surprise, we even saw a group of Montagnais people wearing foreign clothes. There were more people and more trading goods than we had ever imagined.

We looked around until we met another group of Montagnais people. They invited us to build our shelter near them. We all ate together, sharing our caribou and dried fish and their strange, foreign food. We were surprised to learn that they went trapping far into the northwest in the winter and spent all summer at Tadoussac. They no longer hunted caribou or fish. They only hunted beavers. "The beaver does everything perfectly well," joked one of their leaders. "It makes kettles, axes, knives, and bread. It makes everything."

"They are very clever," said my father thoughtfully.

"Yes, and you are too old to change," my mother told him. "Let us go back to our hunting grounds in the woods. Our children will grow clever enough to have the beaver do all their work for them."

Everyone laughed, but I knew we would go back to hunt the caribou, as my mother had said. I wondered whether we would come back to trade for foreign goods at Tadoussac next summer.

They did not hunt caribou or fish anymore. They only hunted beavers.

Caribou, the traditional game animals of the Montagnais, are the only kind of deer in which both males and females grow antlers.

Fur Trade Landmarks

The earliest maps of Canada were drawn from memory.

Maps do more than show where cities and towns are located. They show the distances between places. They also show which parts of the world are water and which are land.

Aboriginal Peoples drew the earliest maps of Canada. Some individuals memorized certain areas of land. When others wanted to travel, the mapmakers drew a map for them in sand or snow. Sometimes they drew maps on bark or animal hides.

European explorers began making maps of North America almost as soon as they arrived. Often, explorers relied on the knowledge of Aboriginal Peoples to help them map the areas they visited. Their earliest maps usually showed only the coastlines. Mapmakers left empty spaces when they were unsure of the features of an area. As the fur trade developed, Europeans ventured inland for the first time. As the fur traders travelled and learned more about the land, they added features to earlier maps drawn by explorers. Fur traders helped map the interior of early Canada.

The following map shows the major regions of the fur trade in early Canada. It also displays the key trading posts that were built between 1530 and 1803.

Grand Banks
- The Grand Banks was the site of Canada's first trade between fishers and Aboriginal Peoples in the early 1500s.

Tadoussac
- Tadoussac was located at the junction of the St. Lawrence and Saguenay Rivers.
- It was an important trading location for Aboriginal Peoples before Europeans came to North America.
- In 1600, Europeans built the first trading post at Tadoussac.

Port-Royal
- Port-Royal was a French settlement founded by Samuel de Champlain in 1605.
- It was located outside of present-day Annapolis Royal, in Nova Scotia.
- Port-Royal was an early site of trade between settlers of New France and local Mi'kmaq peoples.
- Today, Port-Royal has been reconstructed as Port-Royal National Historical Site.

Quebec
- Quebec was founded by Champlain in 1606.
- It was an early trading post on the banks of the St. Lawrence River.
- Quebec became the capital of New France.

York Factory
- York Factory was established in 1684.
- It was the main trading post for the **Hudson's Bay Company**.
- York Factory was located at the mouth of the Hayes River near the Nelson River.
- York Factory was named a National Historic Site in 1968.

Landmarks of the Fur Trade

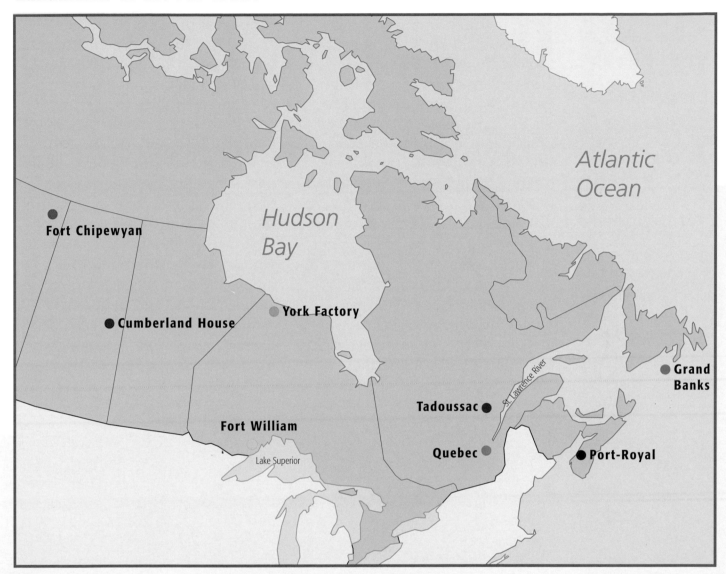

Atlantic Ocean

Fort Chipewyan

Hudson Bay

Cumberland House

York Factory

St. Lawrence River

Grand Banks

Tadoussac

Fort William

Quebec

Port-Royal

Lake Superior

Cumberland House

- Cumberland House was founded by Samuel Hearne in 1774.
- It was the first inland post of the Hudson's Bay Company.
- Cumberland House was built by Cumberland Lake, on the main trade route from York Factory to the Saskatchewan River.

- Its construction began an intense rivalry between the **North West Company** and the Hudson's Bay Company.

Fort Chipewyan

- Fort Chipewyan was founded in 1788 by Roderick Mackenzie.
- It was located near the Athabasca, Peace, and Slave Rivers.

- Fort Chipewyan served as the base for fur trade expansion and exploration into northwest Canada.
- It was the site of many struggles between the North West Company and the Hudson's Bay Company.

Fort William

- Fort William was a trading post of the North West Company.

- It was built in 1803 at the mouth of the Kaministiquia River near Lake Superior.
- Fort William served as the company's major shipping point for furs and trade goods.

Champlain and the Fur Trade

In 1603, French explorer Samuel de Champlain travelled to North America for the first time. As part of a trading expedition, Champlain sailed up the St. Lawrence River and was greatly impressed by the area. Upon his return to France, Champlain informed King Henry IV about the potential for settlement and a profitable fur trade in the St. Lawrence region of North America. He learned that Henry had granted a fur trade **monopoly** to Pierre Du Gua de Monts for 10 years. The monopoly gave de Monts the exclusive right to trade with the Aboriginal Peoples of the area. In return for receiving a monopoly, de Monts was expected to explore the land, establish a colony, and convert Aboriginal Peoples to Christianity.

In 1604, Champlain, de Monts, and about 80 settlers travelled to New France to start a fur trading post. They explored the Bay of Fundy area and chose an island in the mouth of the Ste-Croix River for their settlement. After a hard winter, they learned that this was a poor location. The settlers moved across the bay and built a new settlement called Port-Royal. The French settlers met Mi'kmaq who lived nearby. The French traded

> The settlers moved across the bay and built a new settlement called Port-Royal.

The Iroquois had never seen guns before they fought against Champlain, his men, and the Huron.

Champlain travelled the St. Lawrence River several times. In 1608, he established the settlement of Quebec on a cliff overlooking the river.

with the Mi'kmaq and became their friends, but the Mi'kmaq furs were not enough to pay for the settlement at Port-Royal.

Not everyone in the region respected de Monts' monopoly. Many people traded furs illegally. The king cancelled the monopoly, and Champlain returned to France in 1606. Two years later, he was put in charge of a new expedition to North America. Once again, Champlain travelled to the St.

Lawrence region. At a location along the St. Lawrence River, he built a new fur trading post. He called this post Quebec, after *kebec*, the Aboriginal name for the area, meaning, "where the river gets narrow." It became the capital of New France.

FURTHER UNDERSTANDING

Samuel de Champlain

Samuel de Champlain was a French explorer and mapmaker. He first visited Canada in 1603 on a ship captained by François Gravé Du Pont. Champlain made many of the first drawings and maps of the area. He wrote descriptions of the people he met on his travels and of the places he explored around the St. Lawrence River.

Port-Royal

Samuel de Champlain established the colony of Port-Royal in 1605. In 1607, the colony was abandoned. It was revived by Biencourt de Poutrincourt in 1610, but the British burned it in 1613. Other settlements were tried in the area, but none were permanent. Today, the site is the Port-Royal National Historical Site, near Annapolis Royal, Nova Scotia.

The Fur Trade Wars

Aboriginal Peoples in the St. Lawrence region initially welcomed Europeans to their lands. The Huron, in particular, viewed the French and their weapons as potential **allies** against their enemies, the Iroquois. The Huron and their allies had fought traditional wars of honour against the Iroquois for years before Europeans arrived. Once Aboriginal demand for European trade goods was established, the Huron and Iroquois fought over control of the fur trade.

In 1609, the Huron asked Champlain to join them in a fight against the Iroquois. Champlain agreed because he depended on the Huron for furs. The French joined a group of Algonquins, Montagnais, and Huron in an attack on the Iroquois near Lake Champlain, in what is now the province of Quebec. Their guns terrified the Iroquois, who quickly lost the battle. Champlain and his men participated in several more battles to convince the Huron of their support.

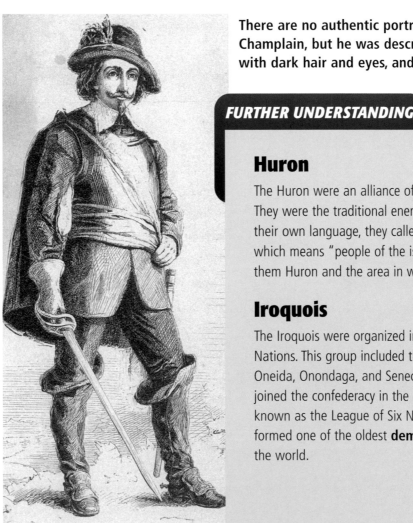

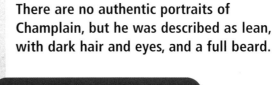
There are no authentic portraits of Champlain, but he was described as lean, with dark hair and eyes, and a full beard.

FURTHER UNDERSTANDING

Huron

The Huron were an alliance of several smaller groups. They were the traditional enemies of the Iroquois. In their own language, they called themselves *Wendat*, which means "people of the island." The French called them Huron and the area in which they lived *Huronia*.

Iroquois

The Iroquois were organized into the **League** of Five Nations. This group included the Cayuga, Mohawk, Oneida, Onondaga, and Seneca. When the Tuscarora joined the confederacy in the early 1700s, it became known as the League of Six Nations. Together they formed one of the oldest **democratic** societies in the world.

Champlain's decision to join forces with the Huron against the Iroquois had terrible consequences. The Iroquois began to dislike the French and formed an alliance with the British, who were settled along the Hudson River. The British encouraged Iroquois hostility toward the French, hoping to eliminate their rivals in the fur trade.

As the fur trade grew, the supply of furs on Iroquois lands began to dwindle. Huron control of the waterways also prevented the Iroquois from trading for furs with nearby Aboriginal groups.

Eventually, the Iroquois sent war parties to try to drive the French out of the St. Lawrence valley. For the next few decades, the Iroquois periodically attacked New France, killing many settlers. They also **raided** the Huron homeland. Armed with a large number of British guns, the Iroquois devastated the Huron, who had much more limited access to European weapons. By the 1650s, many Huron had been killed.

▲▲▲▲▲▲ FIRST-HAND ACCOUNT

Conflict with the Iroquois

Dressed in metal breastplates and helmets, Champlain and two of his men travelled with the Huron to Lake Champlain. The Iroquois and the Huron then met and agreed upon the hour of battle. That night, the Iroquois danced on shore as the Huron sang songs in their canoes. Both sides hurled insults at each other. The next morning, the Iroquois allowed the Huron to land before coming to battle. The Iroquois outnumbered the Huron by more than three to one. Champlain described the short battle in detail.

"Our Indians began to call to me with loud cries...I marched on until I was within some thirty yards of the enemy, who as soon as they caught sight of me halted and gazed at me and I at them. When I saw them make a move to draw their bows upon us, I took aim with my musket and shot straight at one of the three chiefs. With this shot two fell to the ground, and one of their companions was wounded who died a little later. I had put four shots into my musket. As soon as our people saw this shot so favourable for them, they began to shout so loudly that one could not have heard it above the sound of thunder. Meanwhile the arrows flew thick on both sides.

The Iroquois were much astonished that two men should have been killed so quickly, as they had shields of wood which protected them against arrows. This frightened them greatly. As I was reloading my musket, one of my companions fired a shot from within the woods, which astonished them again so much that, seeing their chiefs dead, they lost courage and took to flight, abandoning the field and their fort, and fleeing into the depths of the forest, where I pursued them and shot still more of them."

The Company of One Hundred Associates

> The economy of New France depended on the fur trade, which almost came to a halt during this period.

In 1627, a French business called the Company of One Hundred Associates took control of New France. Unhappy with the colony's progress, the king of France, Louis XIII, gave the company control of the fur trade from present-day Florida to the Arctic Circle and from present-day Newfoundland and Labrador to the Great Lakes and beyond. In return, the company promised to settle 4,000 French settlers along the St. Lawrence River within 15 years. The results of this venture were disappointing.

Continued Iroquois hostility reduced the company's profits and discouraged people from coming to North America. The governor appointed by the company argued with the **clergy**, and the clergy quarrelled with the merchants and the fur traders. The most serious dispute regarded the practice of trading alcohol to Aboriginal Peoples for beaver pelts. The clergy wanted the governor to stop this practice, but the fur traders said it would reduce their profits.

By 1660, the French colony on the St. Lawrence was in a desperate situation. New France was in constant danger from the Iroquois and the British. The economy depended on the fur trade, which almost came to a halt during this period.

Louis XIV wanted New France to become the centre of a mighty empire. When he saw the colony floundering, Louis cancelled the charter of the Company of One Hundred Associates in 1663 and selected his own officials to run the colony.

Cardinal Richelieu created the Company of One Hundred Associates in 1627 in France.

Coureurs de Bois

At the beginning of the fur trade, Aboriginal Peoples brought their furs to European trading posts. Over time, rather than waiting for this to happen, some European fur traders decided to travel into the wilderness to collect furs from the Aboriginal Peoples themselves. These traders were known as *coureurs de bois*, or "runners of the woods." Coureurs de bois left the trading posts in the spring and travelled by canoe into the interior. They brought along supplies and trading items from the posts, and relied on the land for whatever else they needed. When the weather was foul, they built their own shelters. When they needed food, they hunted and fished.

When coureurs de bois met Aboriginal groups, they traded European goods for furs. They stored the furs in their canoes. When they had traded everything they could, the coureurs de bois returned to the trading posts with their canoes loaded with furs.

Coureurs de bois spent a great deal of time learning the ways of the woods from Aboriginal Peoples they met. The Aboriginal Peoples taught coureurs de bois how to build canoes, make clothing out of animal skins, and how to snowshoe. They also pointed out which plants in the woods were safe to eat.

The government of New France did not approve of the coureurs de bois. They wanted the traders to stay in the colony and care for their property, animals, wives, and children. However, coureurs de bois quickly became the standard in the French fur trade. By 1680, there were about 500 coureurs de bois around Lake Superior.

Some waterways in Canada's interior featured many rapids, which could only be crossed by light canoes.

ABORIGINAL WOMEN IN THE FUR TRADE

Aboriginal women played an important role in the fur trade. Many of the fur traders lived with Aboriginal women. These women did much of the work at fur trading posts. Aboriginal women taught the fur traders the languages and customs of their people. Women often acted as interpreters and peacemakers between their people and the traders. This improved trading relationships.

Aboriginal women had many skills that were important to the fur traders. For this reason, they often accompanied traders on trapping and trading trips. Many Aboriginal women acted as guides and mapmakers for the traders. They helped paddle canoes and carried heavy loads across **portages**. When trading parties stopped to rest, Aboriginal women set up camp and prepared meals. They also trapped smaller animals for meat and fur, including rabbits and martens, while European traders searched for beaver.

At the fur trading posts, Aboriginal women looked after fur traders in various ways. They preserved food, collected berries, harvested rice, and made maple sugar. They also dried fish, which could prevent the traders from starving during long Canadian winters. The women knew how to make medicines from plants and nursed traders when they were ill.

Most importantly, Aboriginal women at the posts were responsible for cleaning, dressing, and preserving all the furs before they were sent to Europe for sale. This activity made them indispensible to the fur traders. Their second most important task was preparing pemmican for the traders. Pemmican was the staple food of the fur traders' diet. It was light to carry and did not spoil.

FURTHER UNDERSTANDING

Pemmican

Pemmican, a preserved meat, was a common Aboriginal food. To prepare pemmican, meat was dried in the open air or over a fire. The dried meat was then pounded into a powder and mixed with melted fat. Sometimes berries were added. Once the mixture was cool, it was sewn into buffalo-hide bags. Pemmican could be stored and transported over long distances. European fur traders relied on pemmican for food on their journeys into the wilderness to collect furs. At the trading posts, Aboriginal women performed all of the necessary work involved in making pemmican.

To keep the traders in action, Aboriginal women sewed blankets and fur clothing, including moccasins, for the traders. They made snowshoes and showed Europeans how to walk in them.

The most important form of transportation during the fur trade was the birchbark canoe. Aboriginal women gathered and split the spruce roots that they used to sew the seams of the canoes. They also collected spruce gum, which was used to make the canoes waterproof.

The fur traders learned many skills from Aboriginal women. They learned Aboriginal languages and customs. If a woman from an Aboriginal group lived with a trader, she often acted as an interpreter and peacemaker between her people and the traders, improving trading relationships. The family groups of Aboriginal women were more likely to trade furs with the traders the women lived with. The women also warned the traders of danger from enemy groups. All of these qualities, along with their many skills in the wilderness, made Aboriginal women a very important part of the fur trade.

▼▼▼▼▼▼▼▼▼▼

Aboriginal women were responsible for cleaning, dressing, and preserving all the furs.

Marriage ceremonies between European fur traders and Aboriginal women followed Aboriginal customs. Although not performed in a church, they were considered serious and binding.

Groseilliers and Radisson

Médard Chouart Des Groseilliers and his brother-in-law, Pierre-Esprit Radisson, were coureurs de bois from New France. They began their careers in the fur trade by exploring for furs in the Great Lakes region. Through their interactions with Aboriginal Peoples, the two learned that the lands around Hudson Bay held great prospects for the fur trade.

In 1665, after being arrested by the governor of New France for trading without a license, Groseilliers and Radisson sailed to Great Britain. They told King Charles II about the wealth of furs around Hudson Bay. They asked Charles to set up a fur trading company to trap for furs in the area. With the help of Charles' cousin, Prince Rupert, Groseilliers and Radisson were able to convince the king, some nobles, and several merchants to fund their venture.

On May 2, 1670, the Hudson's Bay Company was created when Charles II awarded the two traders and their investors the right to trade for furs in all the lands

The area surrounding Hudson Bay was named Rupert's Land in honour of Prince Rupert.

drained by rivers flowing into Hudson Bay. Groseilliers and Radisson worked for the company for the next four years, establishing trading posts on Hudson Bay and exploring the lands around it.

In 1674, after a disagreement with the company, Groseilliers and Radisson returned to work for the French. They helped the French trap furs in the Hudson Bay area, which weakened the Hudson's Bay Company. However, in 1684, Radisson and Groseilliers disagreed with France once again. Groseilliers retired from the fur trade. Radisson left New France and was rehired by the Hudson's Bay Company. From 1685 to 1687,

he served as chief trader at Fort Nelson on the Hudson Bay. Radisson eventually retired in Great Britain.

Groseilliers sailed to Hudson Bay on the *Nonsuch.* The Hudson's Bay Company built a replica of the ship in 1970.

The Hudson's Bay Company

King Charles II of Great Britain awarded the Hudson's Bay Company 4 million square kilometres of land to establish the company's new trading area. The area was called Rupert's Land in honour of Prince Rupert, who had helped Groseilliers and Radisson obtain the king's support for their venture.

Over the next 100 years, the Hudson's Bay Company built a network of trading posts along Hudson Bay and James Bay. The trading posts were called factories.

Each post sat at the mouth of a river that flowed into the bay. This made it easy for Aboriginal Peoples to bring their furs to the posts. Rather than venturing into the interior like the coureurs de bois, most British company traders stayed at their trading posts and waited for Aboriginal Peoples to bring their furs to them.

Many people worked at the company factories. The chief factor, the clerk, and often a junior clerk did the trading. Other people, such as doctors, carpenters, and tailors, also

lived at the posts. However, unlike the French, British fur traders did not try to build lasting settlements. The governors of the Hudson's Bay Company were focussed on trading for furs rather than establishing a colony.

With the formation of the Hudson's Bay Company, the French and the British now competed to obtain furs from Aboriginal Peoples.

Henry Kelsey

No European had ever travelled so far west before.

Henry Kelsey was born in Great Britain, where he **apprenticed** with the Hudson's Bay Company as a young man. In 1685, when he was about 17 years of age, Kelsey went to York Factory to work at the trading post. As a clerk, Kelsey became friends with the Cree who came to trade their furs at York Factory. He learned to speak their language and made several trips with them along the coast of Hudson Bay.

In 1690, the Hudson's Bay Company sent Kelsey to invite the Assiniboin to trade at Hudson Bay. Kelsey travelled southwest with a group of Cree returning to their homeland on the prairies, in present-day Manitoba.

After a long journey by canoe, Kelsey reached the borders of Assiniboin country. He spent the winter there with his Cree companions before continuing farther west on foot. In 1691, Kelsey met the Assiniboin at Eagle Lake. He spent two years hunting and travelling the plains with them. No European had ever travelled so far west before. Kelsey was the first European to see buffalo and grizzly bears and to learn of the Rocky Mountains. His travels opened a new trading area for the Hudson's Bay Company.

Kelsey returned to York Factory in 1692. He continued to work for the Hudson's Bay Company for another 30 years.

Henry Kelsey was the first European to see Aboriginal People hunt buffalo on the Plains.

A Cree Boy Visits York Factory

This story is told by an 11-year-old Cree boy who went with his father on a trip to York Factory to trade furs. He describes the ceremony that took place at the trading post.

I could smell the sea and knew we must be close to the British trading post. We had been paddling our canoes, loaded with furs, for many days. We were glad to arrive.

When we could see the post, we shouted and fired our guns as a greeting. A loud boom from the post made me shake. Father explained that the people at the post had returned our greeting with a shot from their cannon.

We landed and set up camp just outside the trading post. I looked for children my own age, but there were none.

I was proud that my father was chosen to lead this trading voyage. I watched as he met the British leader, who was called the chief factor.

Father and the chief factor smoked a peace pipe together for about an hour. Sharing the peace pipe showed the friendship that would exist between them. Then Father and the chief factor took turns giving speeches. Father described our canoes and our furs. The chief factor told us why the British would always be our friends.

Aboriginal Peoples made elaborate weapons with steel and other metals they obtained through trade with Europeans.

The chief factor gave Father a fine set of clothing and other gifts. The rest of us also received gifts. The men got tobacco. I was given a long hunting knife.

The next day, Father gave gifts of beaver pelts to the British. He made another speech. He told the chief factor how far we had come, and he asked the British to trade fairly with us. We sat in a circle, and the men smoked the peace pipe again.

The chief factor then took us to the storeroom of the trading post. Only Father went inside. The rest of us stayed in the trading room. There was a small window in the wall for us to present our furs to the chief factor. Then we chose knives, kettles, cloth, and guns in return for our furs. Father made sure that everything went smoothly.

The chief factor said goodbye. He invited us to come back next year to trade our furs. After loading our canoes with all the goods we had received for our furs, we started the long trip home.

FURTHER UNDERSTANDING

York Factory

York Factory was the Hudson's Bay Company's main trading post. It was built in 1684 on the north shore of the Hayes River near the mouth of the Nelson River. Most Hudson's Bay Company cargo passed through this post. Many Europeans bound for Rupert's Land entered the area through York Factory. The post was operational until 1957. York Factory was named a National Historic Site in 1968.

Pierre de La Vérendrye

The traders built new trading posts for the French as they headed west.

La Vérendrye helped move the fur trade west by building forts as far as the Saskatchewan River area.

Pierre de La Vérendrye was born at Trois-Rivières, in present-day Quebec, in 1685. He joined the military at a young age and fought in several battles before travelling to France. There, La Vérendrye fought in the **War of Spanish Succession**. He received many wounds and, in 1709, was taken prisoner by the enemy army while fighting for France. In 1712, shortly after his release, La Vérendrye returned to Canada.

La Vérendrye was a farmer in New France until 1726, when he joined his brother at the fur trading posts along Lake Superior.

Few furs were left in this area, and the French wanted to search for furs farther west. In 1731, La Vérendrye left a French trading post on Lake Superior and headed west with his sons and his nephew.

La Vérendrye's group travelled toward the fur country in the West. It was a difficult route, with many portages. The traders built new fur trading posts for the French as they headed west. In 1732, La Vérendrye and his family reached Lake of the Woods, in present-day Ontario, where they built a large trading post. Two years later, they reached a spot near Lake Winnipeg where they built a trading post called Fort Maurepas. They continued west along the Saskatchewan River, building new trading posts and collecting many furs.

La Vérendrye and his family traded with Aboriginal Peoples they met. They convinced the Aboriginal Peoples that it was fairer and easier for them to trade with the French than with the British at their posts on Hudson Bay. As a result, the French fur trade grew.

Fur Trade Supplies

Fur traders travelled by canoe on rivers and lakes. Canoes were made of wooden frames covered in sheets of birchbark. The bark was sewn to the frames with tree roots. The canoes were light and could be easily carried, so they were portaged over land when rivers were too difficult to travel. They were waterproofed with spruce or pine tree sap.

River travel could be dangerous. Sharp rocks in the water sometimes punctured the bark. Most fur traders carried supplies to repair their canoes on long journeys.

Traders could begin their trips with hundreds of kilograms of trade goods packed in their canoes. When they met Aboriginal Peoples, they traded these goods for furs. Sometimes, they had to trade for food when their supplies were running low. Major trade goods included cloth and clothing, weapons and gunpowder, cooking pots, and metal tools and utensils. Other items included glass beads, tobacco, mirrors, bells, and combs.

Fur traders also carried navigational equipment on their journeys into the interior. Important instruments included a compass, telescope, and **sextant**. These items helped traders determine where they were and what direction they were travelling.

Each season brought its own challenges. In the late spring, fur traders had to fight off mosquitoes and black flies. In summer, they travelled long distances in the hot sun. When there was rain, they had to stop and wait for the rain to pass, or else their canoes would fill with water and tip over. During winter, traders travelled on foot through deep snow and bitter cold. At any time of the year, weather conditions could change in an instant. Fur traders had to be prepared for anything.

Some fur traders travelled in groups. Hired helpers, called engagés, would paddle great distances and lift heavy loads. When traders had to portage their canoes, engagés carried the canoes and supplies on their backs over rough terrain. Sometimes, they had to walk several kilometres before finding a navigable stretch of river. Engagés also helped set up and build fur trading posts. They carried food supplies and the tools needed to run the forts.

Engagés were strong and agile helpers. They steered canoes to safety through turbulent waters.

The Nor'Westers

The North West Company's coat of arms features the word "perseverance," along with images of the fur trade.

While the British traded at their posts on Hudson Bay, the French continued to trade furs along the St. Lawrence River and west of the Great Lakes.

In the 1750s, the Seven Years' War broke out between France and Great Britain. When the war ended, Great Britain had won control of the French settlements. Some Scottish fur traders in New York decided to move to Montreal to run the fur trade there. The St. Lawrence River was the best route to the fur country.

The Scots and French made good partners. The Scots had money to pay for fur trading trips, and they knew people in Europe who wanted to buy furs. The Scots used the French trading posts and took over the French fur trading companies. They hired many expert French traders, called voyageurs, to trade with the Aboriginal Peoples. Some of the voyageurs had learned to speak Aboriginal languages and had married Aboriginal women. The voyageurs transported the furs back to the merchants. They knew the routes inland to the best fur country. Some voyageurs travelled thousands of kilometres by canoe to explore and trade in areas of Canada where no Europeans had ever been before.

By the 1780s, there were many small fur trading companies in Montreal. They competed with one another. Some of the merchants decided to join together to improve their business. In 1783, they formed the North West Company. The company inherited the traditions of the coureurs de bois. Many Nor'Westers, as the traders working for the company came to be called, spent the winter collecting furs from Aboriginal Peoples.

FURTHER UNDERSTANDING

Seven Years' War

Lasting from 1756 to 1763, the Seven Years' War was the final battle for control of North America. Great Britain and France continued to fight for control of land, the fur trade, and fishing grounds in North America. This war ended in 1763, when the **Treaty** of Paris was signed. France surrendered almost all of its land in North America to the British.

The Montreal merchants found it difficult to get supplies and goods to trading posts in the West. Canoe travel was expensive and took a long time. To solve this problem, in 1803, the Nor'Westers built a large trading centre on Lake Superior called Fort William. Each summer, merchants from Montreal took supplies and trading goods to Fort William. There they met their wintering partners, who came with canoes filled with furs from the inland posts. The Nor'Westers were soon getting twice as many furs as the Baymen, their rivals at the Hudson's Bay Company.

Montreal in the Fur Trade

Explorer Jacques Cartier was the first European to visit the site of Montreal. In 1535, he explored the St. Lawrence River. He found a small Iroquois settlement on an island called Hochelaga. Cartier climbed a nearby hill and named the area Mount Royal, or Montreal. In the summer of 1642, French colonists returned to the location and built a permanent settlement.

The settlers at Montreal soon began a prosperous trade with local Aboriginal Peoples. The location of the settlement made it a central fur trading post. Each summer, Aboriginal Peoples travelled to Montreal to trade their furs for European goods. Later, French traders travelled west from Montreal to collect furs themselves.

After Montreal was surrendered to the British during the Seven Years' War,

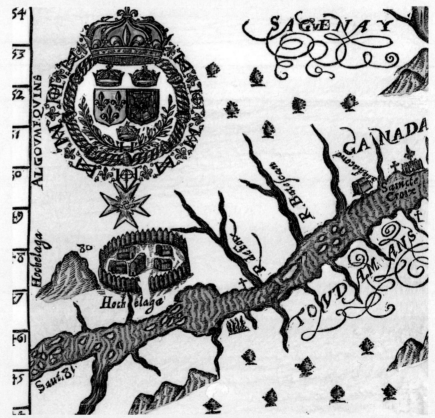

the city remained an important fur trade centre under the control of British merchants. The city served as a base for the formation of the North West Company.

Early maps of New France show Hochelaga as a fortified Aboriginal village. In 1535, Hochelaga was home to about 1,500 Iroquois, but by 1603, these inhabitants had vanished.

THE LIFE OF A VOYAGEUR

Voyageurs were fur traders employed by the fur trading companies of early Canada. The voyageurs inherited the traditions and lifestyle of the coureurs de bois who came before them. They travelled by canoe into the interior to trade for furs with Aboriginal groups. Unlike the unlicensed coureurs de bois, however, voyageurs were licensed to trade. Voyageurs became the typical fur trader in the eighteenth century. They lived lives of adventure and hard work, and often travelled in groups called fur brigades. Here is how one voyageur might have described his life in his journal. What problems did he face?

> The voyaguers inherited the traditions and lifestyle of the coureurs de bois.

June 17, 1792

We are five days' journey away from Fort William. It has been a long, tiring trip for all 10 of us, but especially for me. I am 37, too old for this life. Where are all my friends who became voyageurs with me long ago? They have quit or become worn out. Some have died by drowning or from working too hard.

We travelled a long way today, so we stopped before sundown. We camped in a clearing by the river where there are few mosquitoes. We had been paddling for almost 15 hours. We stopped for 10-minute breaks every hour. That was all that kept me going.

My arms are always sore from paddling. The weight of the pack that

Voyageurs travelled by canoe. In their canoes, they carried trade goods, food, and supplies for craftsmen at trading posts.

I carry on portages makes my back sore, too. Today, as we walked on wet rocks near the rapids, I slipped and fell in the water. Thank goodness it was shallow. If it had been deep, the weight of the pack would have taken me under before my friends could save me.

It is starting to rain again, but the campfire is burning well. I am lying under my overturned canoe, listening to the noise the river makes and my friends laughing and singing.

Why do I love this work? It pays twice what a skilled worker earns in Montreal. I have seen much of this country and met many people. In spite of the hardships, I have had good times with my partners.

The work of a voyageur pays twice what a skilled worker earns in Montreal.

Each summer, thousands of fur traders convened on Fort William. The meeting was known as the "great rendezvous."

FURTHER UNDERSTANDING

Fort William

Fort William was built in 1803, at the mouth of the Kaministiquia River in present-day Ontario. The fort was the North West Company's Lake Superior headquarters and its gate to the West. Until 1821, Fort William was the yearly summer meeting location for the company's Montreal agents and wintering partners. It was also the major shipping point for North West Company furs and trade goods.

Samuel Hearne

Samuel Hearne was born in Great Britain in 1745. He wrote a book about his adventures in Canada, but died three years before it was published.

In the late eighteenth century, fur traders were eager to find a practical trade route to the Pacific Ocean, which would expand their trading rights across the continent. European rulers also encouraged the search for a route to the Pacific, which explorers had been searching for since the late fourteenth century. These European rulers continued to hope that a route west across North America to the Pacific Ocean would make trade with Asia easier. Some even offered a reward to the first person who could discover such a route.

In 1770, the Hudson's Bay Company sent Samuel Hearne to look for a route to the Pacific. Hearne was a British sailor who joined the Hudson's Bay Company as a fur trader in 1766. He set off from the bay on his first expedition in December 1770. Hearne was instructed to search for a route to the Pacific and to investigate a copper mine other travellers had heard about from the local Aboriginal Peoples.

Hearne accompanied an Aboriginal group travelling west from Hudson Bay. They led him overland across a vast, treeless plain known as the Barren Lands. The journey across the plain took 19 months. The guides then led Hearne along the Coppermine River, in the present-day Northwest Territories, where he searched for the fabled copper mine. He found nothing more than one lump of copper. The river, however, led Hearne and his guides to the Arctic Ocean. From there, the group turned south. They crossed Great Slave Lake before returning to Hudson Bay in June 1772. This exploration provided useful information about the lands west of Hudson Bay.

In 1774, Hearne set out on a second expedition. This time, he was charged with founding the Hudson's Bay Company's first inland trading post. Hearne travelled deep into the interior to present-day Saskatchewan, where he founded Cumberland House.

Hearne continued to work for the Hudson's Bay Company until 1787, when he retired and returned to Great Britain. Near the end of his life, he wrote an account of his earlier travels, titled *A Journey from Prince of Wale's Fort in Hudson's Bay to the Northern Ocean.*

Hearne named Great Slave Lake after a Dene Aboriginal group called the Slavey.

FURTHER UNDERSTANDING

Cumberland House

Cumberland House was the first inland post built by the Hudson's Bay Company. It was built on the main trade route from York Factory to the Saskatchewan River, in order to compete against French traders who were intercepting furs from Aboriginal Peoples in the interior. This competition had caused fewer Aboriginal groups to travel to Hudson Bay to trade with the British. The construction of Cumberland House represented a change in Hudson's Bay Company policy, since it was the first time the company ventured into the interior. It signalled a period of intense rivalry with the French fur traders who would later form the North West Company. Cumberland House still stands today. It is the oldest continuously occupied European settlement in Saskatchewan.

Alexander Mackenzie

Alexander Mackenzie led the Nor'Westers' inland expansion. Born in Scotland in 1767, Mackenzie came to Canada at the age of 10 and was educated in Montreal. In 1787, he became a partner in the North West Company and was sent to the company's Fort Chipewyan on the Athabasca River. There, Mackenzie served as second-in-command to Peter Pond, who had explored the region around the fort.

Pond was convinced that the large river flowing west from Great Slave Lake would lead to the Pacific Ocean. Mackenzie was intrigued. In 1789, on the orders of the North West Company, Mackenzie set out to follow the river from Great Slave Lake to its source. Aboriginal Peoples he encountered at the beginning of his journey told him that he would die of old age before he returned and that there were ghastly monsters along the river. Mackenzie decided to continue on his journey anyway. After a difficult trip, he was disappointed to learn that the river emptied into the Arctic Ocean rather than the Pacific. Today, the river is named the Mackenzie River.

In 1793, Mackenzie headed west, following the upper Peace River to the Fraser River. He then travelled overland to the Bella Coola River.

It was an incredible journey. Mackenzie's small party of eight Europeans and two Aboriginal persons climbed perpendicular cliffs and shot whitewater rapids. Finally, the group reached the Pacific Ocean on July 22, 1793. Mackenzie was the first European to cross North America to the Pacific Ocean. He claimed the area north and west of Rupert's Land for Great Britain and acquired a new fur trading area for the North West Company.

Alexander Mackenzie was born in Scotland in 1764. In 1812, he returned to his homeland, where he died in 1820.

After his return from the Pacific, Mackenzie once again worked in the fur trade. He became interested in forming a trading partnership to span the continent. The partnership would involve the union of the North West Company and the Hudson's Bay Company, enabling the British to control a huge portion of the fur trade in North America. His ideas were ignored. Eventually, Mackenzie returned to Great Britain and published a book about his journeys in 1801, entitled *Voyages from Montreal on the River St. Lawrence.*

Mackenzie was the first European to see the Pacific coast of what is now Canada.

FURTHER UNDERSTANDING

Peter Pond

A fur trader from Connecticut, Peter Pond helped to extend the fur trade west when he established a small fort on the Athabasca River, near Lake Athabasca. He developed his theory about a route from Great Slave Lake to the Pacific Ocean from stories told by Aboriginal Peoples in the area. In 1785, Peter Pond was the first explorer to map out the area now known as the Mackenzie Basin. Pond opened up the Lake Athabasca area for the North West Company's fur trade.

Fort Chipewyan

Fort Chipewyan was founded in 1788 by Alexander Mackenzie's cousin, Roderick Mackenzie, who was also a trader with the North West Company. The fort provided easy access to the Athabasca, Peace, and Slave Rivers. It served as the North West Company's base for fur trade expansion and exploration of the northwest interior. Rival fur trading companies struggled for control of the fort and its surrounding area until the 1820s.

People with Different Ideas

Fur traders were constantly competing with each other for furs from Aboriginal Peoples. This is how each of two traders, one from the St. Lawrence River Valley and one from the Hudson's Bay Company, may have tried to persuade an Aboriginal chief to trade with him.

North West Company Trader

Why do you trade with the British? You must carry your furs long distances to their trading posts on Hudson Bay. If they do not want all your furs, you must carry them back to your homes. The British will not even let you into their storehouse to see the goods they have to trade.

You should trade with us. We accept all your pelts. We even travel to your homes to buy them. We give you supplies and do not ask for payment until you have next year's pelts.

Hudson's Bay Company clerks competed with French voyageurs for trading alliances with Aboriginal Peoples.

Hudson's Bay Company Trader

Why do you trade with the French? Their trade goods aren't as good as ours. They cause trouble in your groups.

You should trade with us. Our goods are less expensive. It is worth making the trip to our post to get a fair price for your furs. If you do not want to travel so far, you may trade your furs with the Cree or the Assiniboine. They will bring the furs to us.

Hudson's Bay Company posts were stocked with various European goods to trade with Aboriginal Peoples who brought furs.

Simon Fraser

The river Fraser travelled on, now called the Fraser River, is the longest river in present-day British Columbia.

Simon Fraser was born in 1776 in New York. When he was a child, Fraser's family moved to Canada, and he attended school in Montreal. Some of Fraser's family were involved in the fur trade. In 1792, at the age of 16, Fraser joined the North West Company.

Fraser was sent to a post in the Athabasca region of present-day Alberta. He was a very successful trader. In 1802, Fraser became a partner in the North West Company, and in 1805, he was put in charge of the company's westward expansion beyond the Rocky Mountains.

Between 1805 and 1807, Fraser travelled along the Peace River west of the Rocky Mountains. There, he built a series of forts, including Fort George. In May 1808, Fraser organized an expedition to travel to the Pacific Ocean along what he believed was the Columbia River. Instead, he travelled through previously unknown territory, down what is today called the Fraser River. After a difficult, 36-day journey, Fraser and his men arrived at the Pacific Ocean. They had discovered a new travel route to the ocean. The discovery opened up land beyond the Rocky Mountains for fur trade and settlement.

Fraser returned to Fort George, where he stayed until 1809. From 1810 to 1814, he was in charge of the North West Company's Mackenzie River Department. In 1818, Fraser retired from the fur trade and became a farmer and mill operator.

Changes Caused by the Fur Trade

Aboriginal Peoples of eastern Canada were the first to meet European explorers and traders. Aboriginal Peoples acted as guides for the explorers. They taught the Europeans what they knew about the land. They showed Europeans how to use canoes, snowshoes, and toboggans. The explorers returned to Europe with stories about the new people and lands they had seen. They brought back new food that Europeans had never eaten before, including corn, beans, and squash.

Traders came to Canada to obtain furs. They built trading posts where Aboriginal Peoples could bring their furs. When the fur trade began, it fit with Aboriginal ways of life. Aboriginal Peoples had always hunted and traded for what they needed. The fur trade brought metal tools and weapons that replaced those made of stone and bone. Iron cooking pots and copper kettles replaced those made of clay, skin, bark, or wood. Guns replaced bows and arrows. Hunting for food became quicker and easier.

As the fur trade grew, Aboriginal ways of life changed. For some groups, such as the Mi'kmaq, hunting and trapping for furs to trade

Many European items, such as guns, changed traditional ways of life for Aboriginal Peoples.

replaced summer food gathering and other activities. Aboriginal groups that changed in this way became dependent on European trade goods such as clothing, which was not as warm or well-suited to Canada's climate as the clothing Aboriginal Peoples made themselves from furs and hides.

Instead of hunting only what they needed to survive, Aboriginal Peoples began trapping as many beaver as they could. They began to focus more on European values, such as competition and profit.

The fur trade also changed the organization of Aboriginal groups. Instead of choosing leaders for their wisdom, hunting skills, or bravery, some chiefs were chosen for their skills as competitive fur traders.

Competition between rival fur trading companies caused conflict between the Huron and the Iroquois. The British partnered with the Iroquois, and the French partnered with the Huron. As the British and French fought, so did their Aboriginal trade partners.

The Decline of the Fur Trade

By the 1820s, the struggle for control of the fur trade had taken a toll on both companies.

For 40 years, competition between the Nor'Westers and the Baymen was fierce. Traders from rival companies destroyed each others' forts and ships. They bribed traders to convince them to change their allegiance. They offered more money for furs and did whatever else they could to convince Aboriginal Peoples to trade with their company instead of their rival. At times, the competition for furs even turned violent.

By the 1820s, the struggle for control of the fur trade had taken a toll on both the North West Company and the Hudson's Bay Company. The struggle had damaged both companies, but the North West Company was weaker. To end the fighting, the North West Company merged with the Hudson's Bay Company.

The Hudson's Bay Company became the most powerful organization in the county, with trading posts spanning from coast to coast and legal powers over many settlements that had developed on Hudson's Bay Company lands.

At the same time, the fur trade itself began to change. New ways of treating furs to make felt were invented. Silk hats came into fashion to replace fur hats. Less expensive animals were also found. Within a few years, these changes led to a decrease in the demand for beaver fur. By 1840, the fur trade was shrinking. It was no longer a major industry in Canada.

When the demand for beaver fur decreased, the Hudson's Bay Company expanded into retail, building department stores across Canada.

THANADELTHUR: GUIDE AND PEACEMAKER

The fur trade shaped interaction between Europeans and Aboriginal Peoples for years to come. Many individuals played important roles in developing relationships between the two groups. One was a Dene woman named Thanadelthur, who helped expand the fur trade north and west of Hudson Bay. She might have described her life in the following way.

The fur trade brought many changes to the lives of my people. We began to compete with the Cree people who came into our territory looking for furs.

One spring, a group of Cree attacked our camp. The warriors captured my cousin and me. A year later, we managed to escape. We hid in the forest and trapped small animals for food.

Then the weather turned cold and my cousin died. I followed some tracks that led to the goose-hunting camp of some British traders from Hudson Bay. They took me to a trading post called York Factory.

I lived there over the winter and learned to speak English. I told the chief factor about my people and the rich furs in my homeland. He listened carefully to my stories. He told me that he wanted my people to bring their furs to the Hudson's Bay Company posts. He asked me if I knew how to make peace between the Dene and the Cree.

I thought about the problem. I offered to lead a peace mission to my people.

The chief factor agreed. In the spring, about 150 of us left York Factory. Most of our group were Cree who lived near the post. Our long journey was not easy. Illness forced us to separate. Most people returned to York Factory. Only a few of us arived at the Cree camp.

That is when I took over. I told the Cree that in 10 days I would find my people and bring them to make peace. I left our camp and set off alone for Dene lands. I found a large band of my people a few days later. I talked and talked to get them to believe the Cree wanted to make peace. They finally agreed to come with me.

On the 10th day, we reached the Cree camp. Then I had to persuade the Cree to agree to peace. Finally, both sides smoked a peace pipe. Ten of our people are going to York Factory to become traders and interpreters. My brother and I are going. We will return to our people in the spring.

On your own or with a partner:

1. What skills made Thanadelthur a good guide?
2. What skills helped Thanadelthur succeed as a peacemaker?
3. How did the actions of individuals such as Thanadelthur influence relationships between Europeans and Aboriginal Peoples?

TIMELINE

Events of the past can be shown on timelines. This timeline shows the years 1000 through 1791.

1000
The Norse sail to North America for the first time.

1003
Thorvald Eriksson, a Norse explorer, encounters a group of Aboriginal Peoples in Canada.

1400
European merchants use overland routes to trade with Asia.

1440
New instruments and better maps help sailors find their way across oceans and seas.

1480
The search begins for a sea route to Asia. Some people sail east around Africa. Others sail west across the Atlantic.

1497
Explorer John Cabot reaches the Grand Banks near what is now Newfoundland.

1510
Fishers from Europe begin annual visits to the Grand Banks.

1520
Fishers begin to trade with Aboriginal Peoples along the eastern coast of North America.

1534
Explorer Jacques Cartier explores the Gulf of St. Lawrence and claims the area for the king of France.

1560
Hats made from beaver fur become fashionable in Europe.

1576
Explorer Martin Frobisher explores the coast of what is now Labrador and sails to Frobisher Bay by Baffin Island.

1605
The French start a settlement at Port-Royal. Explorer Samuel de Champlain begins a settlement at Quebec.

1610
Explorer Henry Hudson sails into Hudson Bay. The Huron help Champlain explore inland areas. French farmers settle in the St. Lawrence River valley.

1611
Jesuit missionaries come to Canada to teach Christian beliefs to the Aboriginal Peoples.

1639
Ursuline nuns come to Quebec.

1642
Ville-Marie is founded as a mission post on the island of Montreal.

1649
The Iroquois, Aboriginal allies of the British, wipe out the Huron, Aboriginal allies of the French, in a war for control of the fur trade.

1659
Radisson and Groseilliers explore the area northwest of the Great Lakes.

1670
The Hudson's Bay Company is formed by the British.

1691
Explorer Henry Kelsey reaches the Prairies and sees buffalo.

1713
The Treaty of Utrecht gives Great Britain control over part of eastern Canada and the land around Hudson Bay.

1731
Pierre Gaultier de Varennes et de la Vèrendrye begins exploring west of the Great Lakes and the Prairies.

1750
The British build a fortress at Halifax.

1755
The British expel the French settlers, called Acadians, from Nova Scotia.

1756
The Seven Years' War begins in Europe and spreads to North America.

1758
The French complete construction of Louisbourg, a fortress on Île Royale.

1760
The British destroy the French fortress at Louisbourg.

1763
The Treaty of Paris ends the Seven Years' War. Great Britain takes control of eastern Canada.

1774
The Quebec Act lets French settlers keep their language, religion, and some of their laws.

1783
The American colonies become the United States. Loyalist settlers from the United States move to eastern Canada.

1791
The Constitutional Act divides Quebec into two provinces—Upper Canada and Lower Canada.

ADAM DOLLARD: AN UNSELFISH HERO?

The French and their allies, the Huron and Algonquin, fought the Iroquois many times. They raided each other's lands. They tried to steal each other's furs. During the 1600s, Iroquois sometimes attacked French settlements along the St. Lawrence River.

The story of Adam Dollard's battle with the Iroquois at the Long Sault, a series of rapids on the Ottawa River, has been told many times. In some older history books, Dollard is called a hero. In newer books, his reasons for fighting the Iroquois have been questioned. Here are different versions of his story.

The Basic Facts

Adam Dollard des Ormeaux was a young French soldier. In the spring of 1660, Dollard and 17 friends travelled up the Ottawa River. A small group of Huron and Algonquin people joined them. They all camped near the rapids called the Long Sault.

The next day, a large **fleet** of Iroquois canoes came down the river. Shots were fired. A battle raged for seven days. When the battle ended, Dollard and all his friends were dead.

Quebec Settler

A rumour reached Montreal. An Iroquois force was spending the winter up the Ottawa River. It was part of an Iroquois army that planned to destroy Montreal.

Dollard and his friends decided to strike first. They met the Iroquois at the Long Sault. For seven days, the French and Huron battled the Iroquois from an old Huron fort. Finally, their food, water, and gunpowder ran out.

The bravery of the French impressed the Iroquois. They gave up their plans to attack Montreal and went home.

New Version

Dollard knew that small groups of Iroquois came down the Ottawa River each spring. Their canoes would be full of furs from the North. He hoped to surprise the Iroquois and take their furs.

Dollard's group hid in an old Huron fort near the Long Sault. Instead of traders, a party of Iroquois warriors came down the river. They trapped Dollard and his friends in the fort.

After a long battle, the French lit their last **powder keg**. It fell back and exploded among them, killing them all.

Compare the two versions of the story. Make a chart that lists at least four differences between them. Why might there be different versions of the same event? Which version do you think is correct? What other facts might you need to decide whether Dollard was a hero?

RELIVING THE PAST

The men living at fur trading posts had many different duties besides trapping for furs. They kept stock of supplies, made price lists, and wrote reports for their superiors. The following activities will help you understand what ordinary life was life for fur traders in early Canada.

This chart shows the number of beaver pelts the Hudson's Bay Company charged for certain trade goods in 1720.

Hudson's Bay Company Price List

Trade Goods	Cost
1 gun	14 beaver pelts
5 pounds (2.2 kg) gunpowder	1 beaver pelt
1 hatchet	1 beaver pelt
1 yard (1 m) cloth	3 beaver pelts
1 pound (0.5 kg) tobacco	2 beaver pelts
4 knives	1 beaver pelt
1 kettle	1 1/2 beaver pelts
1 large roll of string	1 1/4 beaver pelts

On your own or with a partner:

1. Which of these goods cost the most?
2. How might the prices of these trade goods have been set?
3. How might these goods have changed Aboriginal ways of life?

In a small group:

1. Choose several members of your class to act as explorers or fur traders. Have each person explain to the class why his or her work was important to the fur trade. Have members of the class vote to decide which person was most important to the fur trade.
2. The Hudson's Bay Company traders had to write reports to company officials in Great Britain. Pretend you are a trader, and write a short report describing how you traded with a group of Cree.

FURTHER RESEARCH

How can I learn more about Canada's fur traders?

Libraries

Most libraries have computers that connect to a database for searching for information. If you input a key word, you will be provided with a list of books in the library that contain information on that topic. Non-fiction books are arranged numerically, using their call number. Fiction books are organized alphabetically by the author's last name.

Internet Resources

The Internet can be an excellent source of information. For more reliable results, look for websites created by government agencies, non-profit organizations, and educational institutions. Online encyclopedias can also be a great source. Avoid personal web pages or sites that are trying to sell something.

Canada: A People's History Online

history.cbc.ca
The online companion to CBC's award-winning television series on the history of Canada, as told through the eyes of its people. This multimedia website features behind-the-scenes information, games and puzzles, and discussion boards. It is also available in French.

The Canadian Encyclopedia Online

www.thecanadianencyclopedia.com
A reference for all things Canadian. In-depth history articles are accompanied by photographs, paintings, and maps. Articles can be read in both French and English.

Exploration, the Fur Trade, and the Hudson's Bay Company

www.canadiana.org/hbc
This website specializes in early Canadian history. Special features include a timeline, stories, and personalities. Articles are available in both French and English.

GLOSSARY

Aboriginal Peoples: the first people who lived in Canada, and those who are descended from them, including First Nations, Inuit, and Métis

allies: people or nations who help each other

apprenticed: assigned to learn a trade by working with someone who specializes in that trade

clergy: people trained to provide religious services

colony: a settlement created by people who have left their own country to settle in another land

democratic: system of government in which citizens rule by voting at public meetings or elect others to represent their interests

documents: something written or printed that provides proof of a fact

extinct: no longer in existence

fleet: a group of boats

Grand Banks: a fishing area southeast of Newfoundland and Labrador

Hudson's Bay Company: a fur trading company controlled by the British

league: a number of people or nations who join together to help one another

merchants: people who buy goods and sell them for higher prices

missionaries: members of religious groups who work to convert others to their religion

monarchs: people who rule countries, such as queens and kings

monopoly: control of a service or product without competition

North West Company: a fur trading company controlled by French and Scottish traders

pelts: the skins of fur-bearing animals

portages: places where travellers carried their boats across land from one lake or river to another

powder keg: a small cask that holds gunpowder

raided: a sudden attack in which the attackers entered land or buildings and seized whatever was inside

resources: things that can be used to meet needs

settlement: a community of people who have moved to a new area

sextant: a tool used in navigation to study longitude and latitude

treaty: a signed agreement between two or more countries

War of Spanish Succession: a war caused by conflicting claims to the Spanish throne, which involved all of Europe in conflict

INDEX

Algonquin 10, 16, 45

Cartier, Jacques 7, 8, 29, 42
Champlain, Samuel de 8, 12, 14, 15, 16, 17, 42
Company of One Hundred Associates 18
coureurs de bois 19, 22, 23, 30
Cree 10, 24, 25, 37, 41, 44
Cumberland House 13, 33

Dene (Chipewyans) 33, 41

explorers 6, 7, 8, 12, 14, 15, 29, 32, 35, 39, 42, 43, 44

Fort Chipewyan 13, 34, 35
Fort William 13, 29, 30, 31
France 6, 8, 9, 14, 18, 23, 26, 28, 42
Fraser, Simon 38

Grand Banks 6, 12, 42
Great Britain 6, 22, 23, 24, 28, 32, 33, 35, 43, 44
Groseilliers, Médard Chouart des 22, 23, 43

Hearne, Samuel 13, 32, 33
Hudson's Bay Company 12, 13, 22, 23, 24, 25, 29, 32, 33, 35, 36, 37, 40, 41, 43, 44
Huron 16, 17, 39, 42, 43, 45
Huronia 16

Iroquois 16, 17, 18, 29, 39, 43, 45

Kelsey, Henry 24, 43

King Henry IV 14
King Louis XIII 18
King Louis XIV 18

La Vérendrye, Pierre, Sieur de 26, 43

Mackenzie, Alexander 34, 35
Mi'kmaq 7, 12, 15, 39
Montagnais 9, 10, 11, 16
Montreal 28, 29, 31, 34, 35, 38, 43, 45
Monts, Pierre Du Gua de 14, 15

New France 8, 12, 14, 15, 17, 18, 19, 22, 23, 26
North West Company 13, 28, 29, 31, 33, 34, 35, 38, 40

Port-Royal 12, 14, 15, 42
Portugal 6

Quebec 9, 12, 14, 15, 42, 43

Radisson, Pierre-Esprit 22, 23, 43
Rupert's Land 22, 23, 25, 34

Seven Years' War 28, 29, 43
Spain 6
St. Lawrence River 8, 9, 12, 14, 15, 18, 28, 29, 35, 36, 42, 45

voyageurs 28, 30, 31, 36

York Factory 12, 13, 24, 25, 33, 41